# BEER & GOOD FOOD

## bob & coleen simmons

TAYLOR TRADE PUBLISHING

Beer & Good Food, a nitty gritty® Cookbook

©2013 by Taylor Trade Publishing
An imprint of
The Rowman & Littlefield Publishing Group, Inc.
4501 Forbes Boulevard, Suite 200
Lanham, MD 20706
www.rowman.com

Produced by CulinartMedia, Inc.
Design: Harrah Lord
Layout: Patty Holden
Photography: Eising Food Photography (all rights reserved)
www.culinartmedia.com

Distributed by National Book Network
1-800-462-6420

ISBN 978-1-58979-885-4
Library of Congress Cataloguing-in-Publication Data on file

Printed in China

# CONTENTS

# THE BASICS

## THE BEER REVOLUTION

We are in the middle of a revolution—a beer revolution. It started very slowly in the '60s, accelerated slightly in the '70s, gathered steam in the '80s and exploded in the '90s.

Beer, like bread, is made from fermented grains. Both predate written history. We can only speculate whether nomadic tribes started settling in one place to raise grain, or started to raise grain after they settled down. The first beers were probably made from bread moistened and fermented by airborne yeasts. Almost every grain-producing culture in history has produced beer.

At the turn of the century, this country produced a lot of good beer. Each immigrant community, whether German, Irish, English or Central European, had at least one small brewery that fashioned beer similar to that made in their homeland. These breweries supplied a small geographic area. Some producers eventually bottled a beer or two, which could be purchased locally, and sometimes regionally.

Prohibition caused many of the breweries to close. Some survived by producing "near beer," or malt syrup, for the home brewer. When Prohibition was repealed in 1933, many breweries found themselves with outmoded equipment, a deficiency of talented brewers and a public that wasn't consuming nearly as much beer as before. The Depression only made things worse. During the dry years, technology and transportation had made great strides. Mechanical refrigeration had become more widespread. The breweries that did survive were often gobbled up by regional breweries, which found it more economical to run a large operation and ship great distances by refrigerated rail car or truck.

World War II created a demand for large quantities of bottled and canned beer for our armed services. Larger breweries could meet this demand and had efficient bottling facilities. The preferred beer seemed to be light in color, high in carbonation, and low in alcohol. It didn't have enough character to offend palates that were not accustomed to the taste of stronger, more flavorful malt beverages. Imported barley and hops were scarce, so corn and rice along with local barley were used to make the beers. After the war, servicemen and tourists returning from Europe longed for the styles of beers they tasted in Europe and a small demand for similar beers began.

Huge advertising budgets were devoted to convincing the public that the lighter style was what beer should be. Many campaigns focused on the brewing water as much as the character of the beer. More and more small and/or regional breweries were acquired by bigger breweries or went out of business. There wasn't a great difference in the major brands. A few of the more robust beers were required to be labeled as "malt liquor" because of the high alcohol content but didn't capture a very large share of the market. Malt liquor was often purchased as much for its added "kick" as for its flavor. Rarely did ads suggest serving beer with a meal.

In the '60s there was a little more time and money, and people started a pattern of more adventuresome eating and drinking. Julia Child found an eager audience, and dedicated individuals started small wineries with a goal of making distinctive, higher quality wines than those being produced by the high-volume standard wineries. The beer industry would soon follow suit.

It took another 20 years for microbreweries to take off. Home brewing had been popular and legal during Prohibition, but waned after repeal. A few adventurous souls continued to brew beer as a hobby. Some made very good beer, but obtaining quality ingredients was difficult. In the early '80s, some of the best home brewers opened bars or restaurants and started selling their beer. In the mid-80s, a few started bottling and selling locally to restaurants and retail outlets. This started the microbrewery explosion.

The best of the brews found an appreciative market. High-quality malt and hops became more readily available, as did information on and equipment for brewing beer. The explosion continues. Every week new "brew pubs" open, and established ones start bottling some of their better brews and move into the microbrewery domain. Major breweries test-market new styles, sometimes under an identifiable name, sometimes with nothing to identify the producer. Poorly managed operations go out of business, but there is always new capital and new talent to fill the marketplace with a wonderful array of interesting, well-made new products.

Who knows where it will all end? We live in very exciting times and as long as one keeps an open mind and a spirit of adventure, the taste delights are endless!

## DEFINING BEER

Beer is usually thought to be a fermented alcoholic beverage made primarily from malted barley or other grains and flavored with hops. However, beer can be defined as any alcoholic beverage made by fermenting grains, and as a result there are several interesting styles of beer being produced today. Beer is usually about 5% alcohol by volume (4% by weight). Its fermentation is produced by mixing yeasts with the grains.

Beer can be divided into two broad styles: ales and lagers. Ales are fermented at a high temperature for a short period of time and the yeast rises to the top of the fermenting liquid.

Ales tend to have complex flavors developed during their warm, quick fermentation, which results in fruity, buttery, and spicy notes in the finished beer. Some ales are bottle conditioned. In this technique, a small amount of sugar is added to the bottle just before capping so that a slow fermentation continues in the bottle, which allows the ale to improve with age. Lagers, on the other hand, are fermented at a lower temperature for a longer period of time, and the yeast tends to settle to the bottom of the fermenting liquid. Lagers have lighter, less complex flavors with malt and hop flavors dominating.

These are not simple cut-and-dry definitions, however. There are myriad exceptions and hybrids. Brewmasters, like winemakers, are artists and are constantly experimenting and striving to make something unusual. Whole books are devoted to exploring beer styles and over 60 distinct styles have been defined. Some of the most common styles on the market follow.

**North American Lager:** Produced by major U.S. and Canadian mega-breweries, this type of beer is pale in color and highly carbonated. The flavor has a hint of malt, a faint bitterness, and often a slightly sweet finish. Use this simple beer in batters, with snacks, as an accompaniment to highly spiced foods, and as a thirst quencher.

**Pilsner Lager:** Similar to North American Lager, pilsner is made with more malt, more hops, and less carbonation. It pairs well with seafood, chicken, and veal dishes with light sauces.

**Dark Lager:** This is made with dark-roasted malt and is fermented at a low temperature using lager yeast. Dark lager has a distinct malty character, but it is lighter and cleaner-tasting than ale. Drink it with pizza, Mexican food, or smoked fish.

**Marzen:** Lagers of this general style are also labeled as *Oktoberfest*, *Dunkel* or *Vienna* beer. These dark beers tend to be maltier and have more character than pilsners. Serve with roast pork, sausages, grilled steak, and hearty pizza.

**Bock:** This lager, traditionally brewed in the springtime, is very malty, dark, sweet, and high in alcohol. It is sometimes highly flavored with hops. Lighter bocks go well with aged cheeses, hamburgers, and full-flavored stews. *Double Bock* and *Triple Bock* have even more malt character and are most often enjoyed by themselves as an after-dinner drink, rather than paired with food.

**Wheat Beer:** Wheat beer is made by replacing a significant portion of the barley malt with wheat or wheat malt during the brewing process. It is made in Belgium, Germany, and the U.S. In Belgium, it is called *wit* (white) beer and in Germany it is called *weiss* (white) or *weisen* (wheat) beer. Serve with grilled chicken, smoked fish, and barbecue.

**Hefe-weisen:** This light-bodied, effervescent lager is brewed with up to half malted wheat. It often has lemon or clove flavors. Most are only lightly flavored with hops and are sometimes quite cloudy. Hefe-weisen is very refreshing as a summer drink and goes particularly well with fish and shellfish.

**Pale Ale:** In North America, this ale has a medium-gold color, a malty flavor, and fruity overtones. It varies widely from producer to producer. Some are lightly hopped, while others heavily hopped and quite bitter. Serve pale ale with barbecued pork or grilled salmon. In England, pale ale is very different. It can range in color from golden brown to copper to very dark brown. "Pale" refers to the fact that it is sparkling clear, never cloudy.

**Bitter:** The most popular beer style in England, bitter is usually served on draft from the tap. It is very similar to English pale ale, which is usually bottled. Both are fruity, full-flavored ales that are delicious with chicken, pork, and vegetarian entrees.

**India Pale Ale (IPA):** This beer is like pale ale, but usually maltier, higher in alcohol, and richer in hop character. It complements beef, lamb, curries, and spicy dishes.

**Amber Ale:** The color of amber ale ranges from medium amber to deep copper. It is maltier than pale ale and is often highly hopped. Its full-bodied, sometimes slightly sweet flavor goes well with roasted poultry, veal dishes, and hamburgers.

**Brown Ale:** Brown ale is a sweet and malty English-style ale. It's delicious with duck and pork dishes, and can be used in salad dressings.

**Cream Ale:** Also called "lager ale," cream ale is warm-fermented in the English manner, then allowed to mellow at lager temperatures. Cream ale is usually very pale in color, sharing qualities of both pilsner and pale ale. Serve it with light dishes, fish, or chicken with light sauces.

**Scotch Ale:** This is a dark version of amber ale with a higher alcohol content. Its strong malty flavors make it a good choice to serve with game, roast beef, ham, smoked poultry, and strong cheeses.

**Abbey or Trappist Ales:** These ales are produced by monastic orders, often with recipes dating back thousands of years. Only six orders still produce beer for the commercial market. These ales are top fermented, bottle conditioned, and have fruity, complex flavors. Serve with rich dishes, game, cheese, or alone.

**Porter:** This very old English-style dark brown ale has pronounced malt flavors. Porter goes well with a variety of meat and cheese dishes.

**Stout:** Darker and heavier than porter, stout is made with highly roasted dark malt, which sometimes lends undertones of coffee or chocolate. Styles range from extremely smoky and bitter, to sweet and almost cognac-like. *Oatmeal Stout* is a light-style stout. Pair stout with oysters, smoked poultry, ham, and cheeses.

**Lambic:** True lambic is naturally fermented in Belgium by wild yeast strains that inhabit the breweries. Most lambics on the market are fruit-flavored and quite intense. Raspberry, cherry, and apricot lambics are worth seeking out. Lambic has only a small amount of hops to allow the fruit's characteristics to show through. Lambics are usually drunk by themselves or incorporated into desserts.

**Celebration Beers:** Typically made once a year for the holidays, these can vary widely from year to year and generally are complex, full-bodied ales, often flavored with spices, herbs, or fruit. They're best savored by themselves.

**Specialty Beers:** In the continuing effort to make something unusual, brewmasters constantly create new types of beers. Smoked beer, hot chile beer, pumpkin beer, and spice beer are a few of the more off-beat examples. Some of the fruit-flavored ales, such as *Weizenberry* and *Honey-Raspberry Ale*, both flavored with raspberries, are delicious. Most of these uncommon beers are better served by themselves instead of with a meal. In small quantities, some can be intriguing and delicious. Try to buy single bottles to taste. You can always buy more if you really like them.

## BUYING AND STORING BEER

Beer, with very few exceptions, is at its best the day it is bottled. In addition to time, heat and light are the enemies of beer. Brown or green bottles protect beer from light, and refrigerated shipping containers protect beer from heat. Beers that are high in alcohol and with pronounced malt and hops tend to stay fresh longer. Recently, large breweries have begun dating each can or bottle of beer, which helps consumers to be certain that the products are fresh. Old, light-struck or "cooked" beer will at the very best have diminished flavor and interest, and at the worst have a metallic taste and a "skunky" aroma. To increase your chances of enjoying fresh beer. here are some hints.

• Buy from a store that sells a high volume of beer. This is especially important when purchasing imported and micro-brewed beer.

• Buy beer from the refrigerator case instead of off the shelf. This assures that for at least part of its life, the beer has been well stored.

• Buy only the quantity that you will drink in a few weeks and, if possible, refrigerate the beer until it is consumed. Failing this, store the beer in a cool, dark place.

• Join a "beer of the month" program. Each month you will automatically receive several bottles of interesting, fresh beer. Beer magazines, food magazines and the internet are all good places to find a program that suits you.

## SERVING BEER

Color, clarity, bubble size, and "head" are the first things one notices about a newly poured beer. A sparkling clean glass is important for this visual inspection. Purists never wash beer glasses with detergent, but we find that glasses washed in the dishwasher with a high-quality dishwasher soap are fine for serving beer. If you hand-wash glasses, be certain to rinse them very well to remove any residue from the detergent. A tablespoon of washing soda in the dishwater will cut oily or soapy films. Air-dry the glasses on a rack, or dry them with a very clean dishtowel.

There are many shapes, sizes, and styles of beer glasses, some of which are traditional to a region, or even associated with a particular brew. Glasses can vary from short to tall, mug-style to stemware, light to heavy, and with hourglass or tulip shapes. All of these styles have their devotees. Our favorite is a generous-sized tulip-shaped wine glass, which shows off the beer's attributes and concentrates the aroma. You can hold the glass by the stem so that the warmth of your hand

does not change the temperature of the beer.

Serving temperature is very important. Serious beer drinkers almost never serve icy cold beer with food. In general, lighter American lager and pilsner should be served cool, at about 40°F to 45°F. Ales should be served a little warmer, about 45°F to 50°F. Porters and stouts are best when drunk a little warmer, about 50°F to 55°F. On a very warm day, serve beer a little cooler, and on a wintry night a little warmer. Remove beer from the refrigerator a few minutes before serving, depending on the temperature of your refrigerator, and let it warm slightly. You may have to let porters and stouts warm for 20 to 25 minutes. Plan on at least 12 ounces per person when serving beer with a meal. Have a few bottles in reserve in case the beer is a great hit.

## TASTING BEER

A great way to entertain is to have a beer tasting. The simplest tastings are very little work and a lot of fun. Select 5 or 6 beers with a theme in mind, and take into account the experience and sophistication of your guests. If they haven't tasted many beers other than North American lager, perhaps select three European lagers and three pale ales. This will lead them gently into appreciating more flavorful beer. The more experienced would appreciate tasting 6 well-selected English ales, assorted porters and stouts, or a group of related microbrews. Summer is the ideal time to taste an assortment of hefe-weisens and wheat beers.

When approaching any unfamiliar beer, you will want to look at it for color and clarity; check the aroma by smelling it; taste it, noticing body and aftertaste; and then decide on its overall quality. As with wine tasting, there is a special vocabulary to describe beer appearance, aromas and flavors.

**Color:** Beer color is primarily dependent on the darkness of the malt used in brewing. American lager colors typically range from pale straw to light gold, with European pilsner ranging a bit more toward medium gold. Ales can be light amber, copper, or medium-brown in hue. Bocks, porters, and stouts are generally medium-brown to almost black in color. A beer's appearance can give an indication of taste, but the darkest beers may not necessarily have the most pronounced flavors.

**Bubble size:** A well-made beer will have very small bubbles that rise to the surface in a steady stream. Inexpensive beers, those that are carbonated to the desired level before shipping, usually have larger, short-lived bubbles. A creamy and long-lasting head (the thick foam that rises to the top of the glass after pouring) is a desirable characteristic.

**Clarity:** Most commercial beers are sparkling clear. Some wheat beers, such as hefe-weisen, are exceptions, as are a few bottle-conditioned ales. The yeast cells, which make a beer cloudy, are filtered out before bottling both for aesthetic reasons and to prevent a secondary fermentation in the bottle during shipping. An unexpected fermentation could change the beer's flavor and possibly produce enough pressure to explode the bottle.

**Aroma:** Beer aromas dissipate rapidly, so sniff the beer immediately after pouring while the head is still forming. Depending on how much and how dark the malt that was used, aromas can range from faintly floral to intensely coffee- or chocolate-like. Hop aromas can be described as floral, grassy, spicy, or citrusy. The variety of hops, the amount used, and when the hops were added during brewing also impact the aroma. Be wary of "off" aromas, as they may hint at unpleasant flavors.

**Flavor:** A beer's flavor comes primarily from the malt, hops, and fermentation by-products. Malt contributes toasty, nutty, roasted, caramel, or coffee-like flavors. Very highly roasted malt can also add a degree of bitterness, as in stouts. Hops provide various degrees of grassy, piney, floral, citrus, and herbal flavors. Fermentation by-products can produce fruity, buttery, or yeasty or alcoholic sensations, as well as unwanted flavors and "off" tastes.

**Body:** Body relates to the textural sensation in the mouth. For example, a light-bodied beer would feel more like water in your mouth, while a full-bodied beer would feel more like milk. Body is largely dependent on unfermented sugars and alcoholic strength.

**Aftertaste:** The aftertaste of beer should be clean, balanced and lingering. Heavier bodied brews tend to have a more pronounced aftertaste.

**Overall quality:** This category is somewhat subjective. Ask yourself: Do I like it? Would I buy it? When would I drink it? Would it accompany food? If so, what food?

Beer goes well with most foods. It can emphasize or contrast with flavors in a particular dish the same way wine does. However, beer is often less expensive and more accessible than wine. Mouth-searing curries, hot chiles, piquant barbecue dishes, and spicy Chinese food cry for a cooling, light, fizzy lager or pilsner. Lemony wheat beers and creamy porters complement grilled seafood and poultry. The Irish consider stout and trout or oysters to be a classic combination. We have included ideas and recipes for wonderfully delicious foods to go with beer. Many of the recipes have beer as an ingredient, and all have been designed to be a better companion for beer than they are for wine. The continuing search for perfect food and beer matches can be a pleasurable lifelong pursuit.

# APPETIZERS

# BEER CHEESE PUFFS

MAKES ABOUT 35 TO 40

These savory little puffs can be served hot out of the oven or cooled slightly. Drink your favorite pilsner or ale.

| | |
|---|---|
| 1 cup amber ale or lager | ¼ tsp. salt |
| ⅓ cup butter | 1 cup flour |
| Pinch cayenne pepper | 4 eggs |
| ½ tsp. dry mustard | ½ cup finely shredded Gruyère |
| ½ tsp. curry powder | or Swiss cheese |

Heat oven to 425°F. Place ale, butter, cayenne, mustard, curry powder, and salt in a small saucepan. Bring to a boil over high heat. Reduce heat to low and stir in flour until well absorbed. Remove pan from heat and add eggs one at a time, beating until incorporated. Stir in cheese. Drop tablespoons of mixture 1 to 2 inches apart on parchment- or foil-lined baking sheets. Bake for 10 minutes. Reduce oven heat to 375°F and bake for 20 to 25 minutes, until lightly browned and crisp. Turn off oven. Remove puffs from oven and make a small slit in sides of puffs with a sharp knife to release steam. Return puffs to oven for 5 to 10 minutes to dry centers. Serve warm.

# MUSTARD-MARINATED SHRIMP

## SERVES 4 TO 6

This popular party appetizer can be made ahead and refrigerated for several hours or even overnight. A prepared specialty beer mustard adds delicious flavor to this dish. Drink a hefe-weisen or pale ale.

1 lb. medium shrimp, peeled, deveined
Boiling salted water
2 Tbsp. spicy brown beer or Dijon mustard
1 large shallot, finely chopped
2 Tbsp. rice vinegar

¼ cup olive oil
½ tsp. red pepper flakes, or Tabasco Sauce to taste
½ tsp. dried tarragon
2 Tbsp. finely chopped fresh parsley
Salt and freshly ground pepper, to taste

Cook shrimp in a generous amount of boiling salted water for 2 to 3 minutes, until they just turn pink and are firm to the touch. Drain immediately and briefly rinse with cold water. Combine remaining ingredients in a small bowl and mix well. Pour over warm shrimp and toss to coat. Cool for 5 to 10 minutes, cover tightly and refrigerate for at least 1 hour before serving. Serve with toothpicks.

## SEAFOOD COCKTAIL SAUCE

MAKES 1 CUP

This is an old-fashioned tomato-flavored dipping sauce. Use it to accompany Shrimp Boiled in Beer or other shellfish.

1 cup ketchup
2 tsp. prepared horseradish sauce
2 Tbsp. lemon juice
½ tsp. Worcestershire sauce
⅛ tsp. celery salt

Combine ingredients in a small bowl. Let stand for 30 minutes to allow flavors to blend.

## SHRIMP BOILED IN BEER

SERVES 3 TO 4

Deveining the shrimp is optional, but it takes less than 20 minutes to tackle a pound of shrimp. Deveined shrimp will absorb more of the beer flavor and the shells will pull off more easily. Add ½ tsp. dried thyme or dill to the shrimp boil if you like. Serve warm or lightly chilled with lots of napkins and Seafood Cocktail Sauce, on left.

1 lb. medium shrimp in shell
2 bottles (12 oz. each) pale ale or lager
1 bay leaf

½ tsp. red pepper flakes
1 tsp. kosher or sea salt
2 Tbsp. lemon juice

Remove shrimp legs. If desired, cut down the backs of shrimp shells with scissors and pull out the interior vein with a toothpick or sharp knife; leave shells in place around shrimp.

Combine ale with bay leaf, red pepper flakes, salt, and lemon juice in a medium saucepan. Bring to a boil over high heat, reduce heat to low and simmer for 5 minutes. Increase heat to high, add shrimp and bring liquid back to a boil. As soon as the shrimp turn pink, about 2 minutes, immediately drain shrimp and pour in a single layer on a large plate or baking sheet to cool. Take care not to overcook shrimp.

# BLUE CHEESE WALNUT SPREAD

**MAKES 1 CUP**

Serve this piquant cheese spread with celery sticks, apple slices, or crackers. Use a food processor to chop the walnuts. This spread can be made a day or two before serving so the flavors have a chance to blend. Drink a mellow stout.

4 oz. cream cheese, room temperature

4 oz. blue-veined cheese, room temperature

2–3 Tbsp. porter or amber ale

3–4 drops Tabasco Sauce

1 cup walnuts, toasted, finely chopped

Mix together cream cheese and blue cheese until smooth and well mixed. Add 2 tablespoons of the porter and Tabasco and mix well. Set aside ¼ cup of the chopped walnuts; mix remaining walnuts with cheese mixture. If mixture is too firm to spread, stir in up to 1 tablespoon porter. Spoon cheese spread into a small crock or bowl and sprinkle with remaining walnuts. Cover and refrigerate for 1 to 2 days. For easier spreading, remove mixture from refrigerator about 1 hour before serving.

# SANTA FE CHICKEN WINGS

MAKES 24

This baked variation of Buffalo chicken wings pairs well with your favorite Mexican beer or lager. Serve with some guacamole and Blue Cheese Walnut Spread, page 17, at your next beer party and provide lots of napkins. The unused wing tips can be used to make homemade chicken stock. Store them in the freezer until needed.

12 chicken wings, or 24 chicken "drumettes"
5 Tbsp. Tabasco Jalapeño Sauce
3 Tbsp. vegetable oil

3 cloves garlic, finely chopped
¼ tsp. salt

Rinse chicken wings and pat dry. If using whole chicken wings, cut off tips and reserve for another use. Cut remaining wing pieces into 2 portions at the joint and trim off excess skin. Combine Tabasco, oil, garlic, and salt in a small bowl. Place wing pieces in a large, locking plastic bag and add Tabasco mixture. Seal bag well and refrigerate for 3 to 4 hours, turning once or twice.

Heat oven to 400°F and line a baking sheet with foil. Remove wings from marinade and place on baking sheet. Bake for 30 to 40 minutes, turning wings over halfway through baking time. Wings should be crisp and brown. Brush wings once or twice during baking with leftover Tabasco mixture. Serve warm.

# SAUSAGES COOKED IN APRICOT ALE

**SERVES 4 TO 6**

This makes a quick appetizer. The fruit-flavored ale gives the sausages a delicious fruity flavor. Serve with a glass of the ale used for cooking or any pale or amber ale.

4 – 5 Italian sausages, mild or hot
1 cup apricot or honey-raspberry ale
1 tsp. brown sugar

Place sausages in a skillet and add ale and brown sugar. Bring to a boil over high heat. Reduce heat to low, cover and simmer for 10 minutes. Turn sausages once or twice and pierce with a fork to release fat. Remove lid, pour out all but 2 to 3 tablespoons liquid, and continue to cook sausages over medium-high heat until nicely browned on all sides. Transfer sausages to a cutting board. When cool enough to handle, slice sausages into ½-inch-thick diagonal slices. Serve with toothpicks.

# LAGER-MARINATED MUSHROOMS

SERVES 3 TO 4

Serve these with toothpicks, toss with salad greens or add to pasta salads. Accompany with an amber ale or dark lager.

1 lb. small button mushrooms
1 bottle (12 oz.) lager
1 Tbsp. sugar
¼ tsp. red pepper flakes
¾ tsp. dried marjoram
½ tsp. salt

1 Tbsp. sherry vinegar
1 Tbsp. olive oil
1 tsp. spicy brown or Dijon mustard
½ tsp. sugar
Salt and freshly ground pepper, to taste
2 tbs, chopped fresh parsley

Clean mushrooms and cut stems even with mushroom caps. If using larger mushrooms, cut in half. Combine lager, 1 tablespoon sugar, red pepper flakes, marjoram, and salt in a 2-quart saucepan and bring to a boil over high heat. Boil mixture for 2 to 3 minutes; add mushrooms and return to a boil. Reduce heat to low and simmer mushrooms, partially covered, for 5 minutes. Remove from heat and cool mushrooms in liquid. Drain cooled mushrooms and place on paper towels to dry.

In a small bowl, whisk together vinegar, olive oil, mustard, ½ teaspoon sugar, salt, pepper, and chopped parsley in a small bowl. Add mushrooms and marinate for 1 to 2 hours in the refrigerator before serving. Remove from refrigerator 30 minutes before serving.

# GARLIC BUTTER

**MAKES ½ CUP**

This simple, flavorful sauce is delicious with Steamed Manila Clams, on right. Sop up any excess with crusty French bread.

2 cloves garlic, finely chopped
½ cup butter

Place chopped garlic and butter in a microwavable bowl. Cook on HIGH until butter melts. Or, place ingredients in a small saucepan and cook over medium-low heat until butter melts. Do not allow garlic to brown.

# STEAMED MANILA CLAMS

**SERVES 4**

These are also delicious in pasta dishes or on pizza. Serve with sliced French bread. Since beer has a tendency to boil over when heated, use a deep-sided pot for this dish. Drink a wheat beer or amber ale.

2 lb. manila clams
¾ cup amber or pale ale
2 Tbsp. minced shallots

4 quarter-sized pieces ginger root
Pinch red pepper flakes
Melted butter, optional

Scrub each clam well with a vegetable brush and place in a large bowl. Discard any open clams. Cover clams with lightly salted cold water and let stand for 30 minutes. If you find a lot of sand in the bottom of bowl, repeat soaking process. Combine remaining ingredients in a deep-sided saucepan with a tight-fitting lid, large enough to hold clams. Bring to a rapid boil over high heat and cook for 1 minute; add clams and cover pan. Steam clams over high heat, shaking pan several times. After 3 to 4 minutes, remove lid and check to see if most clams have opened. Use tongs to transfer opened clams to a bowl. Cover pan and continue to cook for 2 more minutes. Remove remaining opened clams, discarding any that are still unopened. Carefully pour off remaining clear cooking liquid into a measuring cup and distribute among small individual bowls. Serve with small bowls of broth and melted butter or Garlic Butter, on left.

# SPICY INDIAN EGGPLANT SPREAD

MAKES ABOUT 2 CUPS

Drink an India pale ale or Jamaican Red Stripe beer. Use crisp crackers, pieces of chapati, or tortillas as dippers. Garam masala is an Indian spice blend that can be found in Indian markets or specialty food stores.

| | | |
|---|---|---|
| 1 eggplant, about 1 lb. | ½–1 jalapeño chile, seeded, finely chopped | 1 Tbsp. lemon juice |
| 1 tsp. vegetable oil | ½ tsp. turmeric | 1 tsp. toasted sesame oil |
| 2 Tbsp. butter | ½ tsp. ground cumin | Salt and freshly ground pepper |
| 1 small onion, finely chopped | ½ tsp. chili powder | ¼ cup chopped fresh cilantro leaves |
| 2 cloves garlic, finely chopped | ½ tsp. garam masala, optional | |
| 1 inch ginger root, peeled, finely chopped | 2 plum tomatoes, cored, coarsely chopped | |

Heat oven to 400°F. Cut eggplant in half lengthwise and lightly rub skin with vegetable oil. Place eggplant halves cut-side down on an oiled baking sheet and bake for 35 to 40 minutes, until very tender when pierced with a knife. When cool enough to handle, pull skin from eggplant and discard. Scoop out as many seeds as possible and discard. Coarsely chop eggplant pulp and set aside.

Melt butter in a skillet over medium heat and sauté onion for about 8 to 10 minutes, until soft and golden brown. Add garlic, ginger, chile, and spices and cook for about 1 to 2 minutes, until spices release their fragrance. Add tomato pieces and eggplant. Reduce heat to low and cook for 5 to 6 minutes, until tomato is softened. Stir in lemon juice and sesame oil. Check seasonings and add salt and freshly ground pepper. Sprinkle with cilantro leaves just before serving. Serve slightly warm or at room temperature.

# SOUPS & SALADS

# CARROT & LEEK WHEAT ALE SOUP

**SERVES 4 TO 6**

This creamy, orange-colored soup makes a delicious first course or lunch. Use the food processor's 1 mm. slicing blade to cut the carrots easily. The soup freezes well and can be served hot or cold. If you wish, garnish with some finely grated raw carrot.

2 medium leeks, about 1 lb., white part only
2 Tbsp. butter
Pinch red pepper flakes
1 quarter-sized piece ginger root, peeled
Grated peel (zest) and juice of 2 oranges

1 lb. carrots, thinly sliced
1 can (14½ oz.) chicken broth
1 bottle (12 oz.) wheat ale
Salt and freshly ground pepper, to taste
1 Tbsp. honey

Cut leeks in half lengthwise, rinse well to remove sand, and pat dry; slice into ¼-inch half-moons. Melt butter in a large heavy saucepan. Sauté leeks, red pepper flakes, and ginger over low heat for 8 to 10 minutes, until leeks are softened. Add orange juice, carrots, chicken broth, ale, salt, and pepper. Bring to a boil over high heat, cover, reduce heat to low, and simmer for 30 to 40 minutes, until carrots are very tender. Add orange peel and honey and cook for 1 minute. Cool for 10 to 15 minutes. Purée with a blender or food processor until very smooth. Check for seasonings, adding more salt and pepper if needed. Serve in heated soup bowls or refrigerate for 3 to 4 hours and serve cold.

# HEARTY LENTIL SOUP WITH SAUSAGE

**SERVES 6**

This comfort food is perfect for cool-weather meals and even better when made a day or two ahead so the flavors have a chance to blend. Serve with a porter or dark lager.

¼ cup olive oil
1 large onion, finely chopped
2 stalks celery, diced
2 medium carrots, diced
6 cloves garlic, finely chopped
1 tsp. ground cumin
1 tsp. Tabasco Sauce, plus more to taste

1 tsp. dried thyme
1 tsp. dry mustard
¼ cup chopped fresh parsley
1 bay leaf
1 lb. brown lentils, rinsed, sorted
1 bottle (12 oz.) amber or pale ale
1 can (49½ oz.) chicken broth

1 can (14½ oz.) ready-cut tomatoes
1 tsp. salt
Freshly ground pepper, to taste
1 lb. Polish or garlic sausages
Fresh parsley for garnish

Heat olive oil in a 6-quart stockpot over medium heat. Add onion, celery, and carrots and sauté for 6 to 8 minutes, until vegetables soften. Add garlic and cumin and cook for 1 minute. Stir in Tabasco, thyme, dry mustard, parsley, and bay leaf. Add lentils, beer, chicken broth, tomatoes, salt, and pepper. Bring to a boil over high heat. Reduce heat to low, cover and simmer gently for about 35 to 45 minutes, until lentils are tender. Check seasonings, adding more salt, pepper and Tabasco to taste.

Cook sausages on the grill or poach for 5 minutes in simmering water, until heated through. Slice sausages into thin rounds and add to hot soup. Garnish with parsley and serve.

# SPLIT PEA SOUP

SERVES 6

This old-fashioned soup goes well with an Imperial stout or porter. Purée all or part of the soup with a food processor for a smoother texture. Ham hocks vary in saltiness, so don't add salt until you taste the soup at the end.

2 Tbsp. butter
1 large onion, finely chopped
2 cloves garlic, finely chopped
1 stalk celery, finely chopped
1 large carrot, finely chopped
Dash red pepper flakes, optional
1 lb. split peas, rinsed, sorted
1 bay leaf
2 large sprigs fresh parsley

1 lb. ham hocks or ham bone with
    some meat attached
2 bottles (12 oz. each) Holland amber ale
    or hefe-weisen
5 cups water
Freshly ground pepper to taste
Salt to taste
1 tsp. finely chopped fresh mint, for garnish

Heat butter in a large heavy stockpot. Add onion and sauté over medium heat for 3 to 4 minutes. Stir in garlic, celery, carrot, and pepper flakes, if using. Cook for 2 to 3 minutes, stirring constantly. Add remaining ingredients, except for salt and mint and bring to a boil. Reduce heat to low and simmer for 1 to 1¼ hours, until peas are very soft. Remove ham hocks from soup, cool slightly and remove meat from bones. Chop ham finely and return to soup; discard bones. Taste and add salt if needed. Discard parsley stems and bay leaf. Serve soup in warm bowls garnished with mint.

# AVOCADO CITRUS SALAD

SERVES 4 TO 6

This bright winter salad makes a great accent for Jamaican-Style Curried Lamb, page 83, or any grilled meat. Make this just a few minutes before serving so the avocado doesn't darken. Choose a beer that goes well with the main dish.

2 large pink grapefruits
2 large oranges
2 ripe avocados
Salt and freshly ground pepper, to taste

1 small red onion, very thinly sliced,
  separated into rings
2 Tbsp. chopped fresh cilantro

With a sharp knife, cut down sides of fruit to remove peel and white pith. Over a serving bowl, cut down both sides of fruit membranes to release fruit segments. Squeeze any juice remaining in membranes into bowl. Cut each fruit segment into bite-sized pieces and place in serving bowl. Cut avocados into ½-inch cubes and place in serving bowl. Squeeze any juice remaining on the citrus membranes into bowl. Season with salt and pepper and top with red onion slices and cilantro. Toss well and serve immediately.

# GERMAN-STYLE POTATO SALAD

SERVES 4 TO 6

Use thick-sliced smoky bacon in this salad and serve it slightly warm or at room temperature. It is a delicious accompaniment for sausages, grilled meats, or cold cuts from the deli. Cook and peel the potatoes and pour the dressing over them while they are still quite warm.

3 thick slices bacon, cut into ½-inch pieces
1 small onion, finely chopped
2 lb. boiling potatoes, boiled until tender
¼ cup cider vinegar

¾ cup beef broth
Salt and freshly ground pepper, to taste
2–3 Tbsp. finely chopped fresh parsley
1–2 Tbsp. finely chopped fresh chives

Cook bacon in a medium skillet over medium-low heat until browned and crisp; remove from skillet and set aside. Add onion to skillet and cook for 5 to 6 minutes, until onion is soft and translucent. Peel cooked potatoes, cut into quarters and slice thinly. Layer potatoes and bacon in a wide serving bowl, seasoning each layer with salt and pepper. Add vinegar and beef broth to skillet and heat over low heat until just heated through; do not boil. Pour mixture over potatoes and mix gently. Let stand for 15 to 20 minutes, until potatoes absorb liquid. Occasionally tip bowl and spoon liquid over potatoes. Just before serving, sprinkle with parsley and chives.

# GREEN BEAN & MUSHROOM SALAD

**SERVES 8**

This is an easy and delicious year-round vegetable salad. Use high-quality canned green beans if fresh are not available. If using shiitake mushrooms, be sure to remove the stems. Serve with grilled meats or Spicy Braised Chicken Legs, page 62.

1½ lb. green beans, stemmed, cut into
   1½-inch pieces
Boiling salted water
2 Tbsp. olive oil
½ lb. fresh white, cremini and/or
  shiitake mushrooms, sliced

¼ cup thinly sliced green onions, white part only
¼ cup cider vinegar
½ cup diced roasted red bell pepper or pimiento
Salt and freshly ground pepper, to taste

Cook beans in a large pot of boiling salted water for about 10 minutes, until just tender. Drain well and plunge into a bowl of cold water to stop cooking. Drain, pat dry on paper towels, and place in a serving bowl. Heat oil over high heat in a medium skillet and sauté sliced mushrooms for 3 to 4 minutes, until they release their liquid. Add green onions and cook for 1 minute. Add vinegar, heat for another minute, and pour over beans in serving bowl. Toss together. Add red pepper pieces, salt, and pepper and mix well. Serve at room temperature.

# CAESAR SALAD

SERVES 4

A Caesar salad makes a great starter or accompaniment for grilled meats. Be sure to use a good Reggiano Parmesan cheese. When served by itself this goes well with a hefe-weisen or pale ale.

8–10 oz. romaine lettuce leaves
4 slices French or Italian bread
5 Tbsp. full-flavored olive oil
2 cloves garlic, sliced
1 Tbsp. lemon juice

1 tsp. Dijon mustard
1 Tbsp. anchovy paste, or 3–4 canned
    anchovies, drained, finely chopped
Salt and freshly ground pepper to taste
¼ cup freshly grated Parmesan cheese

Wash and thoroughly dry romaine leaves. Wrap with a clean towel and refrigerate. Remove crusts from bread and cut into 1-inch cubes. Heat 2 tablespoons of the olive oil with garlic over medium heat in a large skillet. Remove garlic as it browns and discard. When oil is hot add bread cubes and toss to coat with garlic oil. Cook for 3 to 4 minutes, stirring occasionally, until bread cubes are lightly browned and crisp. Cool on paper towels.

Combine remaining 3 tablespoons olive oil, lemon juice, mustard, anchovy, salt, and pepper in a small bowl and whisk until well blended. Toss lettuce leaves with dressing and sprinkle with Parmesan cheese and croutons. Serve immediately.

# RED CABBAGE & FENNEL SLAW

SERVES 8 TO 10

This colorful salad makes a great accompaniment for barbecued or roasted meats and poultry. Make it a few hours or a day ahead so the flavors have time to blend.

½ cup mayonnaise
¼ cup sour cream
¼ cup lemon juice
2 Tbsp. Dijon mustard
2 Tbsp. sugar
8 cups thinly sliced red cabbage, about 1½ lb.

1 large fennel bulb, trimmed, thinly sliced
3 large carrots, coarsely grated
1 cup roasted unsalted peanuts, chopped
Salt to taste
Generous amount freshly ground pepper

Whisk together mayonnaise, sour cream, lemon juice, mustard and sugar in a small bowl. Place prepared vegetables and peanuts in a large bowl and immediately toss with mayonnaise mixture until thoroughly coated. Season with salt and pepper. Cover and refrigerate for 3 to 4 hours or overnight. Toss again just before serving.

# SPINACH SALAD WITH BLACK BEANS & FETA CHEESE

**SERVES 4**

Here is a zesty salad for lunch, a buffet, or a barbecue spread. The dressing can be made ahead of time, but dress and toss the salad just before serving. Use baby spinach or curly New Zealand spinach if available. Feta cheese often comes packed in brine; if so, drain it before using.

1 lb. fresh spinach, stems removed, or
   8 oz. spinach leaves
1 Tbsp. sherry vinegar
3 Tbsp. full-flavored olive oil
1 small clove garlic, finely chopped
¼ tsp. ground cumin

Salt and freshly ground pepper, to taste
1 can (15 oz.) black beans, rinsed, drained
¼ cup diced roasted red bell peppers
⅓ cup crumbled feta cheese
¼ cup toasted pine nuts or slivered almonds
2 Tbsp. finely chopped fresh mint leaves

Wash spinach leaves well in 2 to 3 changes of water and spin or pat dry. Refrigerate until ready to use. Combine sherry vinegar, olive oil, garlic, cumin, salt, and pepper in a food processor or blender. Process until well mixed. To assemble, place spinach leaves in a large salad bowl with black beans and red peppers. Toss with salad dressing. Add feta cheese and pine nuts and toss. Sprinkle with fresh mint leaves and serve in individual salad bowls.

# BREADS, SIDE DISHES & DESSERTS

# PEPPER JACK CORNBREAD

**SERVES 6 TO 8**

This rich, spicy cornbread is easy to put together and is a delicious accompaniment to barbecue, grilled meat, or egg dishes.

1 cup yellow cornmeal
1 cup all-purpose flour
2 Tbsp. sugar
2 tsp. baking powder
½ tsp. baking soda
½ tsp. ground cumin

1 tsp. salt
1 cup shredded pepper Jack cheese
1 cup buttermilk
3 eggs
3 Tbsp. unsalted butter, melted

Heat oven to 425°F. Generously butter an 8-inch square baking pan. Place cornmeal, flour, sugar, baking powder, soda, cumin, and salt in a bowl and stir well to combine. Add shredded cheese and mix well. In another bowl, whisk together buttermilk and eggs; stir in melted butter. Pour buttermilk mixture over dry ingredients and stir until just combined. Pour batter into prepared baking pan. Bake for 25 to 30 minutes, until nicely puffed and lightly browned. Place pan on a cooling rack and cool for a few minutes before cutting and serving.

# HONEY WHOLE WHEAT ALE BREAD

**MAKES 1 LOAF**

This yeasty bread goes together quickly with a food processor. It makes delicious sandwiches or breakfast toast.

| | |
|---|---|
| 1 bottle (12 oz.) pale ale | 1 pkg. active dry yeast |
| 2 Tbsp. butter | 1 cup stone-ground whole wheat flour |
| 3 Tbsp. honey | 2¾ cups bread flour |
| 2 tsp. kosher salt | Melted butter, optional |

Pour beer into a small saucepan. Add butter, honey, and salt and bring to a boil, stirring well to combine. Remove from heat and cool to about 100°F to 110°F. Stir in yeast until dissolved. Place flours in a food processor and pulse 2 to 3 times to combine. Add ale mixture and process for 2 to 3 minutes until well combined. Spoon dough into a well-buttered 9 x 5 x 4-inch loaf pan, cover with plastic wrap and let rise in a warm place until doubled in size, about 1 hour.

Heat oven to 350°F. Brush the top of bread with a small amount of melted butter if desired. Bake for about 1 to 1¼ hours, until a wooden skewer inserted into the middle of bread comes out clean, or until internal temperature registers 210°F on an instant-read thermometer. Turn bread out of pan onto a cooling rack and cool completely.

# EASY BAKED BEANS

**SERVES 4 TO 5**

These are a terrific accompaniment for grilled meats. Double the recipe if cooking for a crowd.

3 thick slices smoky bacon, cut into
  ½-inch pieces
1 medium onion, chopped
2 Tbsp. molasses
2 Tbsp. brown sugar, packed
1 Tbsp. Dijon or spicy brown mustard

2 Tbsp. tomato paste
1 tsp. Worcestershire sauce
2 cans (15 oz. each) small white beans,
  with liquid
Salt and freshly ground black pepper,
  to taste

Heat oven to 325°F. Sauté bacon pieces in a medium skillet over medium-high heat until soft but not crisp. With a slotted spoon, transfer bacon pieces to a plate. Add onion to skillet and cook over medium heat until soft and translucent, about 10 minutes. Place bacon, onion, and remaining ingredients in a heavy baking dish and mix well. Bake uncovered for 1 hour. If beans are still quite soupy, cook for 15 to 20 additional minutes. Serve hot or warm.

# STUFFED PORTOBELLO MUSHROOMS

**SERVES 6**

This is delicious as a first course, or even as a luncheon or supper entrée. It takes a few minutes to scrape out the dark mushroom "gills," but it results in a more attractive dish. These can be assembled an hour or two ahead and baked just before serving. Panko crumbs are unseasoned Japanese-style dried breadcrumbs that can be found in the Asian foods section of many supermarkets.

6 portobello mushrooms, about 6 oz. each, 4–5 inches in diameter

1 bottle (12 oz.) pale ale

6 Tbsp. butter

8 oz. fresh white mushrooms, trimmed, chopped into pea-sized pieces

2 large shallots, finely chopped

1 Tbsp. sherry vinegar

1 tsp. Worcestershire sauce

1 tsp. dried tarragon

Salt and freshly ground pepper, to taste

2–3 slices prosciutto, finely chopped, optional

²⁄₃ cup panko or dried breadcrumbs

²⁄₃ cup shredded Gruyère or Swiss cheese

1 Tbsp. milk or water, optional

Twist off portobello mushroom stems and reserve. With a teaspoon, gently scrape out dark mushroom "gills" from the underside of mushroom caps and discard. In a large skillet, place mushrooms cap-side down in a single layer and pour in ale. Bring to a boil over high heat. Reduce heat to low, cover and simmer for 12 to 15 minutes, turning mushrooms over once during cooking. Start checking for doneness after 10 minutes. When mushrooms are tender, but still slightly firm when pierced with the tip of a sharp knife, remove from cooking liquid. Discard liquid. Line a rimmed baking sheet with aluminum foil. Place cooked mushrooms cap-side down on foil. Cut off tough ends from mushroom stems and remove a small layer of the woody outside peel. If the center parts are tender, chop into pea-sized pieces and add to chopped mushrooms for stuffing. If entire stem seems woody, discard.

Heat oven to 400°F. Melt butter in a large skillet over high heat. Add chopped mushrooms and sauté for 2 to 3 minutes, until mushrooms release some liquid. Add shallots, vinegar, and Worcestershire and cook for 2 to 3 minutes. Remove from heat, stir in tarragon, and season with salt and pepper. Add prosciutto, panko, and cheese, mixing well. Stir in milk or water if mixture needs more moisture. Mound mixture evenly inside mushroom caps. Press down lightly on stuffing. Bake for 15 minutes, until heated through and top is lightly toasted. If stuffing mixture has cooled, add 5 to 10 minutes to baking time. Serve immediately.

# ALMOND & DRIED CHERRY PILAF

**SERVES 4**

Serve this almond- and fruit-studded rice pilaf with grilled meats, roasted chicken or fish. For a delicious variation, substitute dried cranberries or currants for the cherries, or pine nuts for the almonds. This dish can sit covered for up to 20 minutes before serving.

2 Tbsp. butter
½ cup finely chopped onion
2 whole cloves
1 cup converted rice
1 can (14½ oz.) chicken broth

½ cup pale ale or light-style lager
Salt and freshly ground pepper, to taste
¼ cup dried cherries or golden raisins, coarsely chopped
¼ cup toasted slivered almonds

Melt butter in a heavy medium saucepan. Sauté onion and cloves over medium heat for 4 to 5 minutes, until onion softens. Add rice, stir to coat with butter, and cook until rice turns milky and translucent. Add chicken broth, ale, salt, pepper, and dried fruit. Bring to a boil over high heat. Reduce heat to very low, cover and cook for 20 to 25 minutes, until rice is tender and liquid has been absorbed. Remove cloves and discard. Add almonds and fluff rice with a fork. Remove cloves and discard. Serve warm.

# BEER FONDUE

**SERVES 4 TO 6**

This beer and cheese fondue has a south-of-the-border twist.
Use Mexican beer in the fondue and to drink with it. Celery sticks,
carrot sticks, and blanched cauliflower or broccoli florets also
make delicious dippers. Provide a small plate and a long-handled
fork for each person for spearing bread cubes and/or vegetables.

¾ cup light-bodied Mexican beer, such
    as Corona or Carta Blanca
1 cup shredded sharp Cheddar cheese

1 cup shredded pepper Jack cheese
Tortilla chips or French bread cubes
    for dipping

Pour beer into a heavy saucepan or fondue pot and heat
gently over medium-low heat. Gradually add cheeses and stir
continuously until melted. If not using a fondue pot, pour mixture
into a small heavy casserole and keep warm over a candle or low
flame. Serve with tortilla chips or French bread cubes.

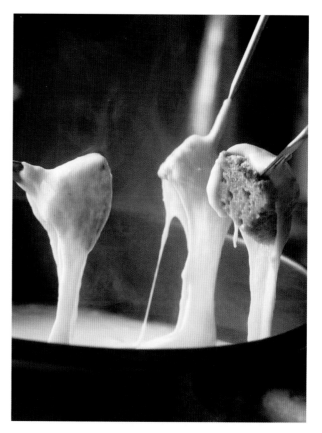

# POTATO GRATIN

SERVES 4

Serve this creamy potato dish with grilled or roasted meats. Soaking the potato slices makes them easy to separate and layer into the baking pan and prevents them from turning brown. Use the food processor's 2 mm. slicing blade for the potatoes. For a variation, sauté 1 large onion or leek in butter and layer between potatoes. Or, add 1 cup coarsely shredded Gruyère or Swiss cheese between potato layers.

| | |
|---|---|
| 1 clove garlic, cut in half | Salt and freshly ground pepper, to taste |
| 2 Tbsp. butter | ¾ cup heavy cream |
| 2 lb. russet potatoes | 1 cup chicken broth |

Rub cut side of garlic clove over a deep-sided 10-inch baking dish. Generously butter the bottom and sides of dish and set aside. Peel potatoes and slice about ⅛-inch thick. Place potatoes in a large bowl, cover with cold water and soak for 30 minutes. Change water 2 to 3 times to rinse off most of the surface starch. Drain potatoes and pat dry.

Heat oven to 375°F. Arrange potatoes in layers in baking dish, sprinkling every other layer with salt and pepper. In a small saucepan, heat cream and chicken broth together until hot to touch; do not boil. Pour mixture over potatoes. Dot top of potatoes with any remaining butter. Bake uncovered for 50 to 60 minutes, until potatoes are tender and top is nicely browned.

# QUICK PEPPERONI PIZZA

**MAKES ONE 13-INCH PIZZA**

Beer and pizza make a delicious twosome. If you are short on time, use a prepared pizza crust from the supermarket and use purchased pizza sauce and well-drained canned mushrooms. Drink a pilsner or dark lager.

4 plum tomatoes, sliced ¼-inch-thick,
   seeds removed
Salt and freshly ground pepper, to taste
6 fresh mushrooms, trimmed, cut into
   ¼-inch slices

Easy Pizza Crust, page 51
¾ cup coarsely shredded mozzarella cheese
1 tsp. dried oregano
2–3 oz. thinly sliced pepperoni

Heat oven to 475°F with a pizza stone if desired. Line a microwave-safe plate with a double layer of paper towels. Place sliced tomatoes on towels, sprinkle with salt and pepper and cook on HIGH for 1½ minutes. Let stand for 5 minutes and blot dry. Using fresh paper towels, cook sliced mushrooms in the same manner as tomatoes.

Roll pizza dough on a work surface to a 13- to 14-inch circle. Spread mozzarella cheese evenly over dough and sprinkle with oregano. Arrange pepperoni pieces, tomatoes, and mushrooms and top with cheese. Bake on pizza stone, or a baking sheet on the lowest oven rack, for about 15 to 20 minutes, until nicely browned and bubbling. Serve hot.

# EASY PIZZA CRUST

**MAKES ONE 13-INCH PIZZA CRUST**

1 cup pale ale
1 pkg. fast-acting yeast
2½ cups bread or all-purpose flour

1 tsp. salt
2 Tbsp. olive oil

For crust, pour beer into a saucepan and heat until just warm to the touch. Place warm beer in a food processor, sprinkle with yeast and pulse until dissolved. Add 1 cup of the flour and pulse. Let rest for 15 minutes; the mixture should be bubbly. Add remaining flour, salt, and olive oil and process for about 1 minute, until dough forms a ball. Dough will be quite soft. Remove dough and place in a lightly oiled bowl. Cover and let rise until doubled in size, about 45 minutes.

Heat oven to 450°F, with pizza stone if desired. Pat, stretch, or roll dough into a 13-inch circle on a piece of parchment or foil. Let rest for a few minutes before adding topping.

# PECAN-PORTER SPICE CAKE

**SERVES 9**

Serve this not-too-sweet cake for coffee, brunch, or with a scoop of ice cream for dessert. It is also wonderful when made with cream ale or stout.

½ cup porter
¼ cup vegetable oil
½ cup molasses
1 cup brown sugar, packed
½ tsp. finely grated ginger root
2 eggs, lightly beaten
1½ cups all-purpose flour

½ tsp. baking soda
½ tsp. baking powder
1 tsp. cinnamon
¼ tsp. nutmeg
¼ tsp. salt
1 cup chopped toasted pecans

Heat oven to 350°F. Oil and lightly flour an 8-inch square baking pan. Pour porter in a small saucepan and bring just to a boil. Remove from heat and pour into a bowl. Add oil, molasses, brown sugar, and ginger and stir with a large wooden spoon until well blended. Add beaten eggs and stir to combine. Mix in remaining ingredients, except for pecans, until batter is smooth. Stir in nuts and pour into prepared baking pan. Bake for 35 to 40 minutes, until top is firm to the touch and a toothpick inserted in the center of cake comes out clean. Remove from oven and cool on a rack.

# SAVORY CHEESE & BREAD PUDDING

SERVES 6

This substantial brunch or supper dish can be made a day ahead.

2 Tbsp. butter
1 large onion, finely chopped
8 oz. white mushrooms, thinly sliced
½ tsp. dried tarragon
Dash red pepper flakes
6–7 cups firm bread cubes, 1-inch cubes
4 thin slices ham, cut into about 1-inch squares

1½ cups shredded Gruyère or Gouda cheese
1⅔ cups half-and-half
⅓ cup amber or pale ale
4 eggs
1 tsp. Worcestershire sauce
1 tsp. Dijon mustard
Salt and freshly ground pepper, to taste

Heat butter in a large skillet over low heat and sauté onion for 6 to 8 minutes, until softened. Increase heat to high and add mushrooms, tarragon, and red pepper flakes. Cook, stirring, for 4 to 5 minutes, until mushrooms have released their liquid and are lightly browned. Butter an 8 x 10-inch baking pan or 12-inch gratin dish and add bread cubes. Top with mushroom mixture, ham pieces, and shredded cheese. Whisk together half-and-half, ale, eggs, Worcestershire, mustard, salt, and pepper. Pour mixture over bread and press down with a spoon to moisten bread. Refrigerate for at least 30 minutes or overnight. Heat oven to 375°F. Bake for 30 to 35 minutes, until puffed. Let rest for 10 minutes before serving. If refrigerated for more than 4 hours, add 10 to 15 minutes to baking time.

# HONEY RASPBERRY ALE-POACHED APPLES

**SERVES 4 TO 6**

Try poaching apples in fruit-flavored beer or lambic. Maple porter also works well. If you like, top apples with a little heavy cream or a scoop of vanilla ice cream.

3 Jonathan, Golden Delicious or other
   cooking apples
⅓ cup brown sugar, packed
1 2-inch cinnamon stick

¼ tsp. nutmeg
Pinch ground cloves
1 bottle (12 oz.) honey raspberry ale

Peel, core, and cut apples into eighths. Combine remaining ingredients in a large heavy 3-quart saucepan and bring to a boil over high heat. Add apples and return mixture to a boil. Reduce heat to low and simmer for 12 to 15 minutes, until apples are tender. Stir occasionally while cooking. Serve hot, warm, or at room temperature.

# STOUT GINGERBREAD

SERVES 9

A full-bodied stout emphasizes the molasses and spice flavors in this old-fashioned gingerbread. Serve with a dollop of whipped cream.

1 bottle (12 oz.) stout or dark ale
6 Tbsp. butter, room temperature
½ cup sugar
¾ cup molasses
2 eggs
2¼ cups all-purpose flour

2 tsp. baking soda
1½ tsp. ground ginger
1 tsp. ground allspice
1 tsp. cinnamon
¼ tsp. ground cloves
¼ tsp. salt

Heat oven to 350°F. Butter an 8-inch square baking pan and lightly dust with flour. Pour stout into a small saucepan and bring to a boil. Cook over high heat for 3 to 4 minutes, until reduced to 1¼ cups. Remove from heat. With an electric mixer, cream together butter and sugar until light and fluffy. Add molasses and eggs and mix until well combined. Sift flour, soda, spices, and salt together. Alternately add small amounts of flour mixture and warm stout to butter mixture, mixing well after each addition. Spoon batter into prepared baking pan. Bake for 45 to 50 minutes, until top is firm and a toothpick inserted in the center comes out clean. Cool on a rack and cut into squares to serve.

# DRIED FRUIT AMBER ALE COMPOTE

**SERVES 4**

Choose dried apples, pears, apricots, peaches, prunes, or mixed dried fruits to make this deliciously sweet dessert. If you like, top with a small amount of vanilla yogurt, whipped cream, or vanilla ice cream. This recipe doubles easily and makes a great brunch dish, too.

1 bottle (12 oz.) amber ale
¼ cup sugar
2 quarter-sized pieces ginger root, unpeeled

1 2-inch cinnamon stick
3–4 whole black peppercorns
1 pkg. (8 oz.) dried fruit

Pour ale into a medium saucepan. Add sugar, ginger, cinnamon stick, and peppercorns and bring to a boil; stir to dissolve sugar. Add dried fruit, cover, reduce heat to low and simmer for 10 to 15 minutes, until fruit is plump and tender. Remove from heat. Cool fruit in cooking liquid before refrigerating. Serve warm, cold, or at room temperature. Remove ginger, cinnamon, and peppercorns before serving.

VARIATION: FRESH & DRIED FRUIT AMBER ALE COMPOTE
After cooking dried fruit, add about 1 cup fresh or frozen blueberries or raspberries, or some orange segments and cook for 1 to 2 additional minutes.

# POULTRY DISHES

# CHICKEN JAMBALAYA

SERVES 4 TO 6

Use spicy smoked Cajun andouille sausage if you can find it. Polish sausage is a good substitute, but precook it to get rid of some of the excess fat. Serve with a porter, bock or your favorite lager.

3 Tbsp. olive oil
8 boneless chicken thighs, skin removed, cut in pieces
2 medium onions, chopped
½ cup diced celery
1½ cups diced red, green and/or yellow bell peppers

2 large cloves garlic, finely chopped
1 tsp. chili powder
1 tsp. dried basil
1½ cups uncooked rice
1 cup diced full-flavored ham
½ lb. andouille sausage, thinly sliced

1 can (14½ oz.) ready-cut tomatoes with juice
2½–3 cups chicken broth
½ tsp. Tabasco Sauce
Salt and freshly ground pepper, to taste
¼ cup finely chopped fresh parsley

Heat oven to 350°F. Heat olive oil over medium-high heat in a heavy ovenproof Dutch oven and brown chicken on both sides; transfer to a plate. Add onions, celery, and peppers to Dutch oven and sauté over medium heat for 10 minutes. Add garlic, chili powder, and basil and cook for another minute. Stir in rice and cook for 3 to 4 minutes, until rice turns translucent. Push rice to one side and return chicken to Dutch oven. Spoon rice over chicken and add ham, sausage, tomatoes, 2½ cups chicken broth, Tabasco, salt, and pepper. Bring to a boil on the stovetop, cover tightly and bake in oven for about 45 to 50 minutes, until rice is tender. Stir rice once or twice during baking and check to see if there is enough liquid. Add a small amount of chicken broth or water if needed. Sprinkle with parsley and serve hot.

## SPICY SALSA

**MAKES 1½ CUPS**

Add salt and pepper just before serving; otherwise, the tomatoes tend to release too much juice.

4 large ripe tomatoes, peeled, seeded, chopped
1 large ripe avocado, diced
4–5 green onions, white part only, finely chopped
2 jalapeño chiles, seeded, finely chopped
½ tsp. dried oregano
1 Tbsp. fresh lime juice
½ tsp. sugar
¼ cup chopped fresh cilantro
Salt and freshly ground pepper to taste

Combine ingredients in a small nonmetallic bowl and refrigerate for about 30 minutes before serving.

## GRILLED CHICKEN SOFT TACOS

**MAKES 8**

Boneless, skinless chicken thighs or breasts are marinated then quickly grilled to provide a smoky flavor to this authentic Mexican taco. Drink a Mexican brew, such as Dos Equis or Negra Modelo, to keep in the spirit. Top with a little guacamole and sour cream if you like.

1 lb. boneless, skinless chicken thighs or breasts
2 Tbsp. fresh lime juice
2 Tbsp. vegetable oil
1 tsp. chili powder
Salt and freshly ground pepper to taste
1 can (15 oz.) black beans

8 corn tortillas, warmed
Spicy Salsa, on left, or your favorite prepared hot or mild fresh salsa
1 cup shredded Cheddar cheese
Fresh cilantro leaves for garnish

Flatten chicken pieces or cut to a uniform thickness. In a bowl, combine lime juice, vegetable oil, ½ teaspoon of the chili powder, salt, and pepper. Add chicken pieces and toss to coat well. Marinate for 30 minutes in the refrigerator. Grill over high heat until nicely browned and juices run clear. Slice cooked chicken into ½-inch strips just before assembling tacos. Heat beans in a small saucepan with remaining ½ teaspoon chili powder. Lift beans out with a slotted spoon and place in a serving bowl. For each taco, place a warm tortilla on a serving plate. Top with a few chicken slices, 1 to 2 spoonfuls of beans, and a small amount of salsa, cheese, and cilantro. Fold up to eat.

# ROASTED CHICKEN WITH GARLIC-GINGER SAUCE

SERVES 3 TO 4

Spoon this mildly spicy sauce over carved roasted chicken pieces. Creamy mashed potatoes or hot rice make a good side dish. Substitute brown ale if maple porter isn't available and drink a pilsner, brown ale or oatmeal stout.

1 frying chicken, about 4 lb.,
    rinsed, dried
Salt
2 quarter-sized pieces ginger root,
    unpeeled
4 cloves garlic, smashed

SAUCE
1 tsp. finely chopped unpeeled
    ginger root
1 large clove garlic, finely chopped
1 bottle (12 oz.) maple porter
2 Tbsp. currant jelly

¼ tsp. red pepper flakes
2 tsp. cornstarch
1 Tbsp. cold water
Salt and freshly ground pepper,
    to taste

Heat oven to 375°F. Lightly sprinkle inside of chicken with salt; add ginger and garlic cloves to cavity. Place chicken on a rack in a roasting pan and roast for 1 to ¼ hours, until a thermometer reads 185°F when inserted into the thickest part of the thigh and the juices run clear when thigh is pierced.

For sauce, combine chopped ginger, garlic, beer, jelly, and hot pepper flakes in a small saucepan. Bring to a boil over high heat. Reduce heat to low and simmer for 5 minutes. About 15 minutes before chicken is done, brush with a small amount of sauce. Transfer chicken to a plate and let stand for 10 minutes before carving. Strain sauce into a saucepan and bring to a boil. Dissolve cornstarch in water and add to sauce. Cook, stirring, until sauce thickens. Season with salt and pepper. Serve hot sauce over carved chicken pieces.

# SPICY BRAISED CHICKEN LEGS

**SERVES 3 TO 4**

These can be made a day ahead, refrigerated, and reheated just before serving. Drink a brown ale or Chinesebeer, such as Tsing Tao.

| | | |
|---|---|---|
| 8 chicken thighs or 10 drumsticks | 2 Tbsp. honey | 2 whole star anise, or |
| 1 orange | 2 Tbsp. cider vinegar | 1 tsp. fennel seeds |
| 1 cup American lager | 2 cloves garlic, thinly sliced | 2 tsp. red pepper flakes |
| 1 cup water | 3 quarter-sized pieces | 2 Tbsp. hoisin sauce |
| ¼ cup soy sauce | ginger root | 2 tsp. sesame oil |

With a vegetable peeler, remove zest from orange in large strips. Squeeze juice from orange and combine with peel, beer, water, soy sauce, honey, vinegar, garlic, ginger root, star anise, and red pepper flakes in a medium skillet with a tight-fitting lid that is large enough to hold chicken pieces in a single layer. Bring mixture to a boil over high heat. Reduce heat to low and simmer for 15 minutes. Add chicken pieces to skillet, cover and simmer for 20 to 25 minutes, until chicken is quite tender. Turn chicken over once during cooking. Remove lid and cool chicken in braising liquid for 20 minutes. Drain chicken; discard liquid. Refrigerate chicken if not eating immediately.

Just before serving, heat broiler. Combine hoisin sauce and sesame oil and brush on both sides of chicken pieces. Place chicken on a rack in a roasting pan and place in oven about 6 inches from heat source. Broil for 3 to 4 minutes on each side, until chicken is nicely glazed and heated through.

# CHICKEN BREASTS WITH MUSHROOM-STOUT SAUCE

**SERVES 4**

Brown or cremini mushrooms have great flavor if you can find them. Drink oatmeal stout porter or amber ale.

4 boneless, skinless chicken
   breasts
Salt and pepper
Flour for dusting
3 Tbsp. olive oil
2 Tbsp. finely chopped shallots

8 oz. small mushrooms,
   trimmed, thinly sliced
1 cup chicken broth
½ cup oatmeal stout or porter
1 tsp. Worcestershire sauce
½ tsp. dried tarragon

1 Tbsp. flour
Salt and freshly ground pepper,
   to taste
2–3 Tbsp. finely chopped
   fresh parsley

Flatten chicken breasts between sheets of plastic wrap to a thickness of about ³/₈-inch. Season with salt and pepper and dust lightly with flour. Add olive oil to a heated skillet and sauté chicken breasts over medium heat for about 2 to 3 minutes on each side, until lightly browned. Transfer to a plate and cover with foil. Add shallots to skillet and cook for 1 minute until softened, but not brown. Add mushrooms, increase heat to high and sauté for 4 to 5 minutes, until most of the liquid is released from the mushrooms. Place chicken broth, stout, Worcestershire, and tarragon in a small saucepan and bring to a boil. Stir flour into mushroom mixture and cook for 1 to 2 minutes. Add boiling broth mixture to mushroom mixture and stir until thickened. Taste for seasoning, adding salt and pepper if needed. Return chicken breasts to pan and top with sauce. Reduce heat to low, cover pan and cook for 10 to 15 minutes, turning chicken over once. Sprinkle with parsley and serve immediately.

# BEER-BRAISED CHICKEN THIGHS

SERVES 4

This tender chicken dish can be made a day before serving. Accompany with buttered noodles or boiled potatoes and some cooked peas or green beans. Drink a brown or Scotch ale.

8 chicken thighs, skin removed
Salt and pepper
Flour for dusting
1 Tbsp. butter
1 Tbsp. olive oil
¼ cup finely chopped shallots
½ cup porter or other dark beer

½ cup chicken broth
1 Tbsp. lemon juice
½ tsp. dried tarragon
⅓ cup heavycream
Salt and freshly ground pepper, to taste
2 Tbsp. finely chopped fresh parsley

Season chicken with salt and pepper and dust with flour; shake off excess. Heat butter and oil in a heavy skillet over medium-high heat and brown chicken on all sides. Do not allow butter to burn. Reduce heat to medium, add shallots and cook for 3 to 4 minutes, until shallots are soft. Add beer, chicken broth, lemon juice, and tarragon and bring to a boil. Reduce heat to low, cover pan and simmer for 10 minutes. Transfer chicken to a plate. Increase heat to high and cook sauce until reduced by about half. Stir in cream and return chicken to pan. Simmer uncovered for 15 to 20 minutes, until chicken is tender. Taste, adjust seasonings, and garnish with parsley.

# ALE-ROASTED CHICKEN WITH CARROTS

SERVES 3 TO 4

Serve with a brown ale or bock, a green salad and some crunchy garlic bread for a satisfying cool-weather supper.

1 frying chicken, about 4 lb., rinsed, dried
Salt
1 lb. carrots, trimmed
2 cups water, plus more if needed
3–4 small onions, cut into quarters

6–8 large cloves garlic
½ cup amber ale
2 Tbsp. butter, melted
1 Tbsp. Worcestershire sauce
½ tsp. finely grated peeled ginger root

Heat oven to 400°F. Season inside of chicken with salt; place on a roasting rack in a large roasting pan with water. Leave carrots whole if they are less than 1 inch in diameter; cut thicker carrots in half. Place carrots, onions, and garlic in roasting pan. Roast for about 1 to 1¼ hours, until a thermometer reads 185°F when inserted into the thickest part of the thigh and the juices run clear when thigh is pierced. Combine remaining ingredients; brush over chicken every 15 minutes while roasting. Stir vegetables once during roasting and add a small amount of water if pan seems dry. About 15 minutes before chicken is done, pour remaining ale mixture over chicken. Let chicken rest for a few minutes before carving. Strain liquid from pan into a cup; skim off fat. Pour into a small pitcher and pass with carved chicken and vegetables.

# TURKEY CHILI VERDE

SERVES 4 TO 6

Turkey chunks are cooked with tomatillos, white beans, and spicy jalapeños in this savory stew. Serve with hot tortillas and your favorite Mexican brew.

2 Tbsp. vegetable oil
2 large onions, finely chopped
4 large cloves garlic, finely chopped
3–4 jalapeño chiles, seeded, finely chopped
2 Tbsp. ground cumin
1 tsp. dried oregano
1 lb. turkey tenderloins or breast pieces,
    cut into ⅜-inch cubes

1 can (7 oz.) whole roasted green chiles,
    drained, seeded, chopped
1 can (12 oz.) whole tomatillos with juice,
    coarsely chopped
2 cans (14½ oz. each) chicken broth
1 cup light Mexican beer, such as Corona
1 tsp. salt
2 cans (15 oz. each) small white beans
¼ cup coarsely chopped fresh cilantro

Heat vegetable oil in a heavy stockpot. Sauté onions over medium-low heat for 8 to 10 minutes, until softened. Add garlic, jalapeños, cumin, and oregano and cook for 1 to 2 minutes. Add turkey, green chiles, tomatillos, chicken broth, beer, and salt and bring to a boil. Reduce heat, partially cover and simmer for 25 minutes. Purée 1 can of beans and their liquid with a food processor or blender. Drain remaining can of beans. Add puréed and whole beans to stockpot and heat through. Garnish with cilantro and serve in soup bowls.

# TURKEY MUSHROOM MEATBALLS

MAKES 36

Serve these with mashed potatoes or polenta to catch the rich beer sauce. Drink a bock or amber ale. Use the food processor to chop the mushrooms. You can also make these into smaller cocktail-sized meatballs and serve with toothpicks for a party.

½ cup fresh breadcrumbs, crusts removed
½ cup milk
7 Tbsp. butter
4 green onions, white part only, finely chopped
4 oz. white mushrooms, stemmed, finely chopped
2 cloves garlic, finely chopped
1 lb. ground turkey
1 egg, lightly beaten
½ tsp. dried thyme
½ tsp. dry mustard
Freshly grated nutmeg, to taste
Salt and freshly ground pepper, to taste
2 Tbsp. finely chopped fresh parsley
3 Tbsp. flour
1¼ cups chicken broth
1¼ cups amber ale or American lager
2 Tbsp. soy sauce
2 Tbsp. tomato paste

Combine breadcrumbs with milk in a small bowl; set aside. Heat 2 tablespoons of the butter in a large skillet over medium heat. Add onions, mushrooms, and garlic and sauté until moisture has cooked out of mushroom mixture. Remove from heat. Squeeze milk from breadcrumbs and discard milk. Add soaked breadcrumbs to mushroom mixture and mix well. Cool. In a large bowl, combine ground turkey, egg, thyme, mustard, nutmeg, salt, pepper, and parsley. Add cooled mushroom mixture and mix well. Form mixture into ¾-inch balls.

Wipe out skillet, add 2 tablespoons of the butter and melt over medium heat. Sauté a few meatballs at a time in butter until lightly browned on all sides; transfer to a plate. When all meatballs are browned, add remaining 3 tablespoons butter and flour to skillet. Scrape up browned bits from the bottom of pan and pour in chicken broth, beer, soy sauce, and tomato paste. Slowly bring mixture to a boil, stirring constantly. Adjust seasonings. Return meatballs to pan, cover and simmer for 20 minutes over low heat. Serve hot.

# MEAT DISHES

# PORTER-BRAISED BEEF BRISKET

**SERVES 8 TO 10**

Serve this slow-cooked pot roast on a cold evening with garlic mashed potatoes, buttered noodles or polenta, and some caramelized carrots. Drink a porter or brown ale. Use the leftover meat to make terrific sandwiches.

3 cups thinly sliced onions

1 beef brisket about 4½ lb., fat trimmed

1 tsp. salt

Freshly ground pepper to taste

1 Tbsp. Worcestershire sauce

2 Tbsp. tomato paste

1 tsp. dry mustard

4 large garlic cloves, smashed

1 bay leaf

1 cup porter or amber ale

¼ tsp. red pepper flakes

1 Tbsp. cornstarch dissolved in
   2 Tbsp. water, optional

Heat oven to 350°F. Place half of the onions in a heavy baking dish with a tight-fitting lid. Place brisket on top and season with salt and pepper. Combine Worcestershire, tomato paste, and mustard and spread over brisket. Add remaining onions, garlic, bay leaf, beer, and pepper flakes. Cover tightly and bake for 3 to 3½ hours, until meat is very tender. Remove meat and slice thinly across the grain. Arrange on a serving platter with onions. Strain pan juices into a small saucepan and skim and discard as much fat as possible. For a thicker sauce, bring pan juices to a boil in a small saucepan. Add a small amount of dissolved cornstarch and cook for 2 to 3 minutes until sauce reaches desired consistency, adding more if necessary.

# BEEF, BEER & ONION STEW

**SERVES 6**

Bacon, onions and beer flavor this classic beef stew from Belgium. Serve with boiled or mashed potatoes and drink a Belgian Duvel or Trappist ale.

4 oz. thick-sliced bacon, cut into 1-inch pieces

3 lb. lean chuck or shoulder beef, cut into 1-inch cubes

4 large onions, about 2 lb., thinly sliced lengthwise from stem to root

2 cloves garlic, finely chopped

1 bottle (12 oz.) dark ale or porter

1 bay leaf

1 tsp. dried thyme

1 Tbsp. Dijon mustard

1 Tbsp. brown sugar

½ tsp. salt

Freshly ground pepper, to taste

Cook bacon pieces in a large skillet over medium heat until some fat is released and bacon is translucent, but not brown. Transfer bacon to a heavy 4- to 6-quart casserole or stockpot. Increase heat to high and brown beef cubes a few at a time in skillet until nicely browned on all sides. Place browned meat in casserole with bacon. Reduce heat to low; cook onions in skillet for 8 to 10 minutes, until onions are soft and lightly browned. Scrape up browned bits from bottom of skillet. Add garlic and cook for 1 to 2 minutes. Add remaining ingredients, bring to a boil and pour over beef cubes. Simmer stew covered over low heat for 1 to 1½ hours, until beef is tender.

# GRILLED KOREAN BEEF IN LETTUCE PACKAGES

SERVES 3 TO 4

Ask your butcher to slice the meat very thinly. If you wish to slice the beef yourself, place it in the freezer for an hour before cutting—partially frozen beef is much easier to slice. Makes a great lunch or informal appetizer. Drink an Asian beer or India pale ale.

3 Tbsp. soy sauce
1 Tbsp. rice vinegar or dry sherry
1 tsp. toasted sesame oil
¼ tsp. Tabasco Sauce
1 Tbsp. brown sugar

1 clove garlic, crushed
1 tsp. finely minced peeled
    ginger root
8–10 green onions, white
    part only

1 lb. thinly sliced beef sirloin or
    eye of round, about ⅛-inch
    thick, cut across the grain into
    2 x 3-inch pieces
8–10 large iceberg lettuce leaves
1 avocado, cut into ½-inch cubes

Place soy sauce, rice vinegar, toasted sesame oil, Tabasco Sauce, brown sugar, garlic, and ginger root in a blender or food processor and process until smooth. Pour into a nonmetallic bowl. Slice 2 of the green onions thinly and add to bowl with sliced meat, stirring to coat meat with marinade. Cover and marinate at room tem-perature for 20 to 30 minutes. Cut remaining green onions into thin matchstick strips; place in a bowl of ice water until crisp. Drain onions and pat dry just before serving.

Heat grill to high. Drain meat and discard marinade. Grill for 1 to 2 minutes on each side, until just cooked through. Do not overcook. To serve, place 1 to 2 slices hot grilled meat on a lettuce leaf and top with cubes of avocado and a few green onion strips. Fold over one end of lettuce leaf and roll up cigar fashion.

# GRILLED FLANK STEAK ADOBO

**SERVES 4 TO 5**

The chipotle chile in the marinade gives this steak a distinctive smoky character. Use canned chipotles in adobo sauce, which can be found in the Mexican food section of the supermarket or in specialty food stores. Serve with. a crisp green salad and Easy Baked Beens, page 43, or Potato Gratin, page 49. Drink an oatmeal stout or porter. To make sandwiches the next day, lightly warm meat in the microwave and place on some good bread that has been generously spread with mustard. Include some roasted red bell pepper strips for flavor and color.

1 flank steak,about 1½ lb., well trimmed
1 canned chipotle chile plus 1 Tbsp. adobo sauce
1 clove garlic, finely chopped
2 Tbsp. vegetable oil

2 Tbsp. soy sauce
Juice of 1 lime
½ tsp. dried oregano

Place flank steak on a plate. Remove and discard stem and seeds from chile and chop finely. Place chile and adobo sauce in a small bowl. Add garlic, oil, soy sauce, lime juice, and oregano and mix well. Spoon mixture on both sides of steak and marinate at cool room temperature for 35 to 45 minutes. Grill on a hot grill or barbecue fire for about 6 minutes on the first side and 4 minutes on the second; beef should be pink in the middle. Transfer to a plate, cover loosely with foil and let rest for 10 minutes before carving. Holding knife at a 45-degree angle, slice thinly across the grain. Serve immediately.

# SAUERBRATEN

SERVES 6 TO 8

Start marinating the meat
3 to 4 days in advance to get
the classic piquant taste of this
German dish. Serve with potato
pancakes or noodles, and a
brown ale or German lager.

MARINADE
1 large onion, chopped
1 carrot chopped
1 stalk celery, chopped
2 whole cloves
1 bay leaf
5–6 peppercorns
5–6 juniper berries
1 cup dry red wine
½ cup red wine vinegar
2 cups water

2½–3 lb. eye of round or top
   round roast, well trimmed
Salt and pepper
Flour for dusting
¼ cup vegetable oil
½ cup finely chopped onion
½ cup finely chopped carrot
½ cup finely chopped celery
2 Tbsp. flour
2 Tbsp. tomato paste
½ cup crushed gingersnaps
Salt and freshly ground pepper,
   to taste

Combine marinade ingredients in a saucepan and bring to a boil. Remove from heat and cool to room temperature. Place roast in a large locking plastic bag or nonreactive bowl just large enough to hold meat. Add cooled marinade. Seal bag well or cover bowl securely and refrigerate for 3 to 4 days, turning meat over each day. Marinade should cover meat.

When ready to cook, remove meat from marinade. Strain marinade, reserving liquid and discarding solids. Pat meat dry. Season meat with salt and pepper and dust with flour. Heat oil over high heat in a large heavy Dutch oven and brown meat well on all sides. Transfer meat to a plate. Reduce heat to medium and sauté finely chopped onion, carrot, and celery for about 5 to 6 minutes, until soft. Sprinkle flour over vegetables and cook for another 2 minutes. Return reserved marinade to Dutch oven and stir well. Return meat to Dutch oven and bring liquid to a boil over high heat. Cover, reduce heat to low and cook for about 2½ hours, until meat shows no resistance when pierced with the tip of a knife. Transfer meat to a platter and cover with foil to keep warm. Pour cooking liquid through a strainer into a saucepan and discard vegetables. Bring liquid to a boil over high heat and add tomato paste and crushed gingersnaps. Reduce heat to medium and cook, stirring frequently, for 5 to 6 minutes, until sauce is smooth and thickened. Taste sauce and add salt and pepper if needed. To serve, slice meat and coat with sauce.

# PORK CHOPS WITH BEER-CAPER SAUCE

**SERVES 6**

Boiled new potatoes or steamed rice and buttered carrots complement chops served in a creamy piquant sauce. Drink a merzen or India pale ale.

2 Tbsp. butter
6 pork loin chops, about ¾-inch thick
1 Tbsp. flour
1 Tbsp. Dijon mustard
½ cup beef broth

½ cup pale ale
Salt and freshly ground pepper, to taste
⅔ cup sour cream
2 tsp. capers, rinsed, drained
¼ cup finely chopped fresh parsley

Heat butter in a large heavy skillet over medium-high heat and brown pork chops for about 2 minutes on each side. Remove chops from skillet. Stir flour and mustard into pan drippings and cook for 1 minute. Gradually stir in beef broth, ale, salt, and pepper until mixture is smooth and comes to a boil. Return chops to skillet. Reduce heat to low, cover, and simmer for 10 to 12 minutes, until chops are cooked through and tender. Stir in sour cream and capers and heat gently, but do not boil. Taste and adjust seasonings. Sprinkle with parsley and serve immediately.

# ROASTED PORK WITH BROWN ALE SAUCE

**SERVES 6 TO 8**

Serve this as the main course for a company dinner with oven-roasted potatoes and carrots. If you have leftover roast make sandwiches on rye bread with spicy brown mustard and dill pickle slices. Drink a golden or brown ale.

3 lb. boneless pork loin, fat trimmed to a thin layer
Salt and freshly ground pepper
2 Tbsp. soy sauce
1 clove garlic, finely chopped
1 quarter-sized piece ginger root, peeled, finely chopped

1 Tbsp. brown sugar
½ cup water
1 cup brown ale or honey porter
1 cup chicken broth
12–16 dried prunes
1 Tbsp. cornstarch dissolved in 2 Tbsp. cold water

Heat oven to 350°F. Rub pork roast with salt and pepper. Combine soy sauce, garlic, ginger, and brown sugar in a small bowl and spoon over pork. Place pork in a roasting pan with water. Roast for about 1½ hours, until pork reaches an internal temperature of about 165°F. Transfer pork to a platter and cover with foil. Pour ale and chicken broth into pan, bring to a boil on the stove top and scrape up brown bits from the bottom of pan. Remove from heat. Strain pan juices into a small saucepan and skim and discard fat. Add dried prunes and simmer over medium heat for 5 to 10 minutes. Stir in dissolved cornstarch and cook for 2 to 3 minutes, until thickened. Adjust seasonings. To serve, slice pork and spoon sauce and prunes over individual servings.

# OVEN-ROASTED SPARERIBS

SERVES 2 TO 3

These meaty brown spareribs are basted with a beer marinade. Bake some potatoes the last hour of roasting and serve with Green Bean and Mushroom Salad, page 34. Drink an amber or pale ale. If you like a sweeter, tomato-based barbecue sauce on your ribs, follow the recipe; then, brush ribs with your favorite purchased sauce and bake for another 5 to 10 minutes.

3 lb. pork spareribs
¼ cup cider vinegar
Salt and freshly ground pepper
1 cup lager
⅓ cup brown sugar, packed
2 tsp. brown or Dijon mustard

2 tbs. soy sauce
1 tsp. hot Hungarian paprika
2 Tbsp. tomato paste
1 Tbsp. vegetable oil
Salt and freshly ground pepper, to taste

Heat oven to 375°F. Line a baking pan with foil and spray a roasting rack with nonstick cooking spray and place in pan. Place ribs on rack, sprinkle with 2 tablespoons of the cider vinegar and season with salt and pepper. Roast for 1½ to 1¾ hours, until ribs are brown and meat pulls away from the bone.

While ribs are roasting, combine remaining 2 tablespoons vinegar and other ingredients in a bowl. After 30 minutes of roasting, turn ribs over and baste with marinade. Turn and baste ribs every 15 minutes. Serve hot or reheat before serving.

# JAMAICAN-STYLE CURRIED LAMB

SERVES 6

Drink a Samuel Smith's pale ale or a Jamaican Red Stripe lager with this spicy curry. Serve with lots of steamed rice and Avocado Citrus Salad, page 31. Ask the butcher to slice the leg of lamb into 1-inch pieces through the bone.

4 1b. shank-end leg of lamb, cut into 1-inch pieces, or 3 lb. lamb stew meat
1 Tbsp. vegetable oil
2 large onions, chopped
3 cloves garlic, finely chopped
2 tsp. finely chopped ginger root

1 habanero chile, or 4 jalapeño chiles, seeded, finely chopped
3 Tbsp. curry powder
1 can (14½ oz.) ready-cut tomatoes
1 can (14½ oz.) chicken broth
Water

1 bay leaf
1 tsp. salt
Generous amount freshly ground pepper
1 Tbsp. red wine vinegar
1 Tbsp. butter, optional
1 tbs, flour, optional

Trim excess fat from lamb. Heat vegetable oil in a large heavy 5- to 6-quart stockpot or Dutch oven. Over high heat, brown lamb cubes on all sides, a few at a time. Transfer browned pieces to a platter. Reduce heat to low, add onions and stir to scrape up brown bits on the bottom of pan. Sauté onions for about 8 to 10 minutes, until soft and golden, about 8 to 10 minutes. Add garlic, ginger, chile, and curry powder and cook for 1 to 2 minutes to release flavors. Return meat to pan and add tomatoes, chicken broth, and enough water to barely cover meat. Add bay leaf, salt, and pepper. Bring to a boil over high heat. Reduce heat to low and gently simmer uncovered for 1 hour. Test meat for doneness; it should be very tender. Skim fat from the surface of stew and discard. Add vinegar and cook for another minute.

If you desire a thicker sauce, melt butter in a small saucepan, add flour and cook for 1 to 2 minutes. Spoon in about 1 cup cooking liquid from stew and cook, stirring, until mixture starts to thicken. Add mixture to pot with lamb and cook for 3 to 4 minutes, until stew thickens.

To serve, pour stew into a serving dish.

# HAM WITH APRICOT ALE SAUCE

SERVES 4

Ham pairs deliciously with a dried apricot-ale sauce. Serve with Potato Gratin, page 49, and fresh steamed asparagus.

2 Tbsp. butter
2 Tbsp. minced shallots
⅓ cup finely chopped dried apricots
1 Tbsp. lemon juice
2 tsp. brown sugar
½ cup chicken broth

½ cup apricot or pale ale
Pinch mace or powdered ginger
Pinch cayenne pepper
2 tsp, cornstarch dissolved in 1 Tbsp. cold water
1 ham steak, about 1 lb., or other cooked ham, heated

Melt butter in a small saucepan. Add shallot and sauté over medium heat for 1 to 2 minutes, until softened. Add remaining ingredients, except cornstarch and ham, and bring to a boil over high heat. Reduce heat to low and simmer for 5 minutes. Add a small amount of the cornstarch mixture and continue to cook until sauce thickens to the consistency of heavy cream. Add more cornstarch mixture if needed. Slice ham into serving pieces. Spoon sauce over ham.

VARIATION: HAM WITH CHERRY-WHEAT ALE SAUCE
Substitute cherry wheat ale for apricot ale and dried cherries for dried apricots.

# SEAFOOD DISHES

# THAI SHRIMP CURRY

**SERVES 4**

Serve this spicy, creamy curry over hot steamed rice and drink a pilsner or Thai beer, such as Singha.

1 cup hefe-weizen or wheat beer
3 jalapeño chiles, seeded, finely chopped
4 cloves garlic, finely chopped
2 tsp, grated peeled ginger root
1 Tbsp. paprika
½ tsp. turmeric
1 tbs, ground coriander
½ tsp. ground cumin
1 Tbsp. sugar

1 can (14 oz.) unsweetened coconut milk
Grated peel (zest) and juice of 1 lime
Salt and freshly ground pepper, to taste
2 tsp. cornstarch mixed with 1 Tbsp. cold water
1 lb. large shrimp, peeled and deveined
Coarsely chopped fresh cilantro leaves for garnish
Hot steamed rice

Combine beer, chiles, garlic, ginger, paprika, turmeric, coriander, cumin, and sugar in a medium saucepan. Bring to a boil over high heat. Reduce heat to low and simmer for 15 minutes. Add coconut milk, lime peel, lime juice, salt, and pepper and return to a boil. Stir in cornstarch mixture and cook for 2 to 3 minutes, until sauce thickens. Add shrimp and cook for about 3 minutes, until shrimp turns pink. Adjust seasonings. Sprinkle with cilantro leaves and serve over hot rice.

# CHINESE-STYLE SWEET & SOUR FISH

**SERVES 4**

Serve this dish with hot steamed rice to catch the delicious sauce. Rock cod, sea bass, swordfish or other firm-fleshed fish works well. Drink a Tsing Tao or another Asian beer.

1– 1 ½ lb. firm fleshed skinless fish fillets
Salt and pepper
Flour for dusting
¼ cup vegetable oil
1 bunch green onions, white part only, cut into matchstick strips

2 jalapeño chiles, seeded, cut into matchstick strips
2 quarter-sized pieces ginger root peeled, finely minced
1 clove garlic, finely chopped
½ cup chicken broth
1 Tbsp. soy sauce

1 Tbsp. dry sherry or Shao Xing rice wine
½ tsp. Tabasco Jalapeño Sauce
2 tsp. cider vinegar
2 tsp. brown sugar
1 tsp. toasted sesame oil
1 Tbsp. cornstarch dissolved in 2 Tbsp. cold water

Cut fish fillets into 1-inch cubes, sprinkle with salt and pepper, and lightly dust with flour. Heat a large skillet that will hold fish in a single layer over medium heat and add vegetable oil when hot. Gently stir-fry fish for about 5 minutes, until lightly browned. Transfer fish to a platter. Discard all but 1 tablespoon oil from skillet. Add onions, chiles, ginger, and garlic and sauté for 1 minute. Add chicken broth, soy sauce, sherry, Tabasco, vinegar, brown sugar, and toasted sesame oil and bring to a boil. Return fish to pan and simmer for 1 to 2 minutes. Pour in about half of the dissolved cornstarch mixture and stir until thickened. Sauce should be the consistency of heavy cream. Add a little more dissolved cornstarch if necessary.

# RED SNAPPER PROVENÇAL

**SERVES 4**

Pair this fish in garlicky tomato sauce with steamed rice and a golden lager or pilsner.

¼ cup full-flavored olive oil

½ cup chopped onion

½ cup finely chopped fresh fennel, including some feathery tops

3 cloves garlic, finely chopped

4 plum tomatoes, seeded, chopped

⅓ cup amber or pale ale

Grated peel (zest) and juice of 1 orange

1 Tbsp. tomato paste

¼ cup coarsely chopped kalamata or other brine-cured black olives

1 Tbsp. drained capers

¼ tsp. dried tarragon

4 red snapper fillets or other firm fish fillets, about 6 oz. each

Salt and freshly ground pepper, to taste

Flour for dredging

Heat 2 tablespoons of the olive oil in a heavy saucepan or skillet. Sauté onion and fennel over medium-low heat for 10 to 12 minutes. Add garlic, tomatoes, beer, orange juice, and tomato paste and cook over medium-high heat for about 8 to 10 minutes, until juice from tomatoes is released and sauce thickens slightly. Remove from heat and add olives, capers, tarragon, orange peel, salt, and pepper; keep warm.

Lightly dust fish with salt, pepper, and flour. Heat remaining 2 tablespoons olive oil over medium-high heat in a large skillet. Sauté fish for about 3 to 4 minutes on each side, until nicely browned. Spoon sauce over fish and serve immediately.

# SEA BASS WITH LEMON-CAPER SAUCE

SERVES 4

Firm-fleshed sea bass, halibut or swordfish steaks are cooked to moist perfection using this simple method. Serve with a wheat beer or ale.

4 sea bass or other fish steaks, about
    8 oz. each, 1–1½ inches thick
Salt and freshly ground pepper
Flour for dusting
1 Tbsp. vegetable oil
¼ cup chicken broth
¼ cup light-bodied lager or ale

1 Tbsp. butter
1 Tbsp. lemon juice
1 Tbsp. stone-ground mustard
2 Tbsp. drained capers
1 tsp. cornstarch dissolved in
    2 tsp. cold water or beer
Salt and freshly ground pepper, to taste

Heat oven to 425°F. Pat fish dry with paper towels, season both sides with salt and pepper and lightly dust with flour. Heat oil over medium heat in an ovenproof skillet large enough to hold fish steaks in a single layer. Just before oil starts to smoke, add fish and sauté for 2 minutes. Turn fish over and cook for 1 minute. Place skillet in oven and bake until fish flakes easily, about 7 minutes. While fish bakes, bring chicken broth and beer to a boil in a small saucepan and cook until reduced to ⅓ cup. Stir in butter, lemon juice, mustard, and capers. Add cornstarch mixture, bring to a boil and cook until sauce thickens. Season with salt and pepper.  Remove fish from skillet, blot with paper towels, and serve with sauce.

# BEER-BATTERED FRIED SHRIMP OR FISH

SERVES 2 TO 3

This easy beer batter is also great for vegetables. Make the batter at least 2 hours ahead. Use a good thermometer to make sure the frying oil is at the proper temperature. Don't fry too many pieces at one time and let the oil return to temperature before frying the next batch. Serve with Red Cabbage and Fennel Slaw, page 37 or Caesar Salad, page 35.

1 cup all-purpose flour
²⁄₃ cup plus 2 Tbsp. lager or pale ale
½ tsp. salt
1 tsp. baking powder
Pinch cayenne pepper

¼ tsp. paprika
4 cups peanut or corn oil
1 lb. shrimp, peeled, deveined,
    butterflied, or 1 lb. fish fillets cut
    into 1 x 3-inch "fingers"

Whisk together ²⁄₃ cup of the flour, ²⁄₃ cup beer, salt, baking powder, cayenne, and paprika in a small bowl and let stand at room temperature for at least 2 hours. Just before using, whisk in remaining 2 tablespoons beer and pour batter into a shallow dish or pie plate. Place remaining ⅓ cup flour in another shallow dish. Pour oil into a heavy deep-sided pan and heat until a deep-fat thermometer registers 375°F. Lightly dust shrimp or fish with flour, coat with batter and let excess drip off for a few seconds. Fry a few pieces at a time in hot oil until golden brown. Drain on paper towels. Serve hot.

## CAPER SAUCE

**MAKES ABOUT 1 CUP**

½ cup mayonnaise
½ cup sour cream
1 Tbsp. Dijon mustard
2 tsp. lemon juice
3 Tbsp. capers, drained, coarsely
    chopped
Generous amount ground white pepper
2 tsp. finely chopped fresh chives

Combine ingredients in a small bowl and mix well. Chill until ready to serve.

## BEER-POACHED SALMON STEAKS WITH CAPER SAUCE

**SERVES 4**

Beer makes a flavorful poaching liquid for individual fish steaks or a larger piece of fish. Serve the cooked fish hot or cold with Caper Sauce, which can be made ahead and refrigerated.

1 bottle (12 oz.) hefe-weizen or wheat beer
1 lemon, thinly sliced
2–3 green onions, coarsely chopped
1 quarter-sized piece ginger root, unpeeled
1 sprig fresh thyme
1 bay leaf

3–4 whole peppercorns
¼ tsp. salt
4 salmon steaks, about 1-inch thick
Finely chopped fresh parsley, for garnish
Caper Sauce, on left

In a skillet large enough to hold fish pieces in a single layer, combine beer, lemon, green onions, ginger, thyme, bay leaf, peppercorns, and salt. Bring liquid to a boil over high heat. Reduce heat to low and simmer for 10 minutes. Slide fish into liquid, cover and simmer over low heat for 8 to 10 minutes, until salmon has turned opaque and is slightly springy when pressed. Line a platter with paper towels; remove cooked fish from liquid and place on paper towels to drain. Blot liquid from top of fish. Place salmon steaks on individual serving plates, sprinkle with parsley and serve hot, warm or cold with Caper Sauce.

# FISH TACOS WITH SPICY CABBAGE SLAW

MAKES 10

Hefe-weisen or pilsner pairs perfectly.

2 cups finely shredded green cabbage
½ cup coarsely grated carrot
½ cup matchstick-sized strips red bell pepper
4 green onions, white part only, finely chopped
1 small jalapeño chile, seeded, finely minced
1 cup finely chopped pineapple, mango or orange pieces
2 Tbsp. mayonnaise
2 Tbsp. sour cream

2 Tbsp. lemon juice
½ tsp. prepared horseradish
Salt and freshly ground pepper, to taste
10 preformed regular-sized taco shells
2 Tbsp. vegetable oil
1 lb. thin fish fillets, such as sole, orange roughy, or flounder
Salt and pepper flour for dusting
Fresh cilantro leaves for garnish

Combine cabbage, carrot, red pepper, onions, jalapeño, and pineapple in a salad bowl. Mix together mayonnaise, sour cream, lemon juice, horseradish, salt, and pepper in a small bowl. Pour dressing over vegetable mixture and toss to coat vegetables.

Warm taco shells in a hot oven according to package directions. Season fillets with salt and pepper and lightly dust with flour. Heat oil in a nonstick skillet over medium heat until quite hot. Sauté fish for about 3 minutes on each side. Fish should be cooked through, but still moist. Remove fish and cut into ½-inch pieces. Serve in warm taco shells with cabbage slaw and garnish with cilantro leaves.

# SICILIAN-STYLE GRILLED FISH

**SERVES 4**

A garlic and oregano marinade spices up halibut, sea bass, snapper, or other firm fleshed fish. Serve with a wheat beer or pale ale, a crisp salad, and baked potatoes.

½ cup olive oil
3 Tbsp. lemon juice
2 cloves garlic, finely minced
1½ tsp. dried oregano

3 Tbsp. finely chopped fresh parsley
Salt and freshly ground pepper, to taste
4 fish fillets, about 6 oz. each

Combine olive oil, lemon juice, garlic, oregano, parsley, salt, and pepper in a small bowl and whisk until well combined. Place fish fillets on a plate or in a nonmetallic pan and coat with marinade. Marinate for 20 minutes.

Heat grill to medium. Remove fish from marinade and grill for 3 to 4 minutes on each side.

# INDEX